ΥΚΗΗΚΛΑΣΦΑΛΤΙΤΙΣΑΙΜΑ
ΡΑΘΑΛΑCCΑ

ΒΗΟΥΕ

ΤΟΥΒΑΓ
ΠΠΟΥ ΕΝΘΑΛΕΓΕ
ΒΕΘΩΡΑ CΙΒΑΠΤΙ
CΘΗΝΑΙΚΑΝ
ΔΑΚΗΝΤΟΝΕΥΝΟΥΧΟ

ΙΟΥΔΑ
ΤΟΤΟΥΑΓΙΟΥ
ΖΑΧΑΡΙΟΥ

ΒΗΘΛΕΕΜ
CΩΧΩ
ΒΕΘΖΑΧΑΡ

ΕΦΡΑΘΑ
ΡΑΜΑ ΦΩΝΗ
ΕΝΡΑΜΑ
ΗΚΟΥCΘΗ

ΜΟΡΑΣ
ΘΕΝΗ
ΧΑΙ
ΑCO
ΠΡΟ

CΑΦΙΘΑ

ΑΚΕΛ
ΑΜΑ
ΕΚΟΡΕΝ
ΓΤΟΥΠΡΟ
ΒΑΤΑ
ΙΩΒΗΝΥΝ

ΝΙΚΟΠΟΛΙC

ΤΟΑΝΝΑΒΑ ΓΕΔΟΥΡΗΚ
ΙΑΤΡΟΑ
ΠΟΛΙC

ΓΑΒΝΗΛΗΚΑΙΠΛΗΝΙΑ ΑΚΚ
ΗΝΤΝΕ

ΕΝΕΤΑΒΑ

THE
LAND
OF
JESUS

THE LAND OF JESUS

ALVIN N. ROGNESS

based on original research
by Jean Roger

PHOTOGRAPHY
GARO NALBANDIAN

Augsburg Publishing House
Minneapolis, Minnesota

1976 First American Edition,
Augsburg Publishing House
© 1974 Sadan Publishing House, Ltd.,
Tel Aviv, Israel
Library of Congress Catalog Card No. 76-1389
International Standard Book No. 0-8066-1531-1

Scripture quotations unless otherwise noted are from the Revised
Standard Version of the Bible, copyright 1946, 1952, and 1971 by
the Division of Christian Education of the National Council of
Churches.

Manufactured in Israel

THE LAND OF JESUS

Palestine is a small country, at the crossroads of three continents — Asia, Africa, and Europe. Powerful nations of the past used it as a corridor of traffic from east to west. Intermittent wars between empires ravaged its cities and countryside. Again and again its people were driven into exile.

The excellence of a painting is not measured by the size of its canvas, nor is the significance of a country determined by square miles. This is the piece of earth God chose as a bridgehead for his invasion of the world to recover his children. In no corner of the world has such unparalleled power for good been unloosed.

God's strategy of recovery began with Abraham. He led him and his family out of the fascinating civilization of Ur in Chaldea, let them wander as nomads in the Fertile Crescent, in Galilee, Samaria, and Judea, and finally settled them in the Negev Desert in the region of Beersheba. To Abraham and his son Isaac and his grandson Jacob he gave the promise that through them and their descendants all nations would be blessed. From this family God sent the Messiah, Jesus Christ, and from this family came the early apostles to proclaim the good news of salvation throughout the Mediterranean world.
This little strip of land is cherished by three great world religions — Judaism, Christianity, and Islam — each reaching back to Abraham as its patriarch.

In the very first book in the New Testament, Matthew traces the genealogy of Jesus back to Abraham. Luke is bolder still, going beyond Abraham to Adam himself, and identifying Jesus with the whole human race, as well as with the "chosen people," the Israelites. Jesus belongs to all mankind, even though he is of the tribe of Judah and the house of David.

Whether a person is an archaeologist, a sociologist, an historian, or a simple observer, this land provides endless interest. Excavations yield clues to the past, almost from the beginning of mankind, through the Bronze and Iron ages, up to the more recent Byzantine and Crusader periods. Perhaps in no part of the world have there been as many "digs."

6

When in 1947 the decision of the United Nations created Israel as a sovereign state, this corner of the world again became a center of international attention. Since then Jewish refugees and immigrants from more than 90 countries around the world have found their way to their ancient "home." It is not surprising that ancient tensions between Arabs (who through Ishmael also trace their origins back to Abraham) and Jews should increase and threaten the peace of the new government, and even the world. Who but the Jews themselves can understand the exhilaration they feel upon returning to the land of their fathers? After 2000 years of longing and countless persecutions and continual praying, they at long last have national boundaries of their own. Despite the obvious strides that have been made in industrialization and in reclaiming arid land for forests and grazing, for fruit and grain, the rivalries between these two proud peoples continue to press for solution.

Most of the visitors who come year after year are not students of archaeology or of politics. They are ordinary people who have grown up with the Bible and who long to see with their own eyes the places that have become dear to their imaginations. Not since the Crusades of the 12th and 13th centuries have so many people from the West, notably from the United States, visited the homeland of Jesus. They are enthralled by the names of hills and valleys and towns that take them back into the centuries long ago.

THE DEAD SEA SCROLLS

The most exciting archaeological discovery of recent times was made quite accidentally by a young Bedouin shepherd who stumbled upon the now famed Qumran scrolls in the hills of the Jebel Qarantal area near the Dead Sea. These scrolls provide a link between the Old and the New Testament periods. They record the life of a Jewish sect known as the *Essenes*. These people seem to have been completely separated from normative Judaism whose center was the Temple in Jerusalem. Leading a life of prayer and penance, they lived in expectation of redemption close at hand. Even before the discovery, the Essenes had been made known to us by authors of old, such as

Josephus Flavius, Pliny the Elder, and Philo of Alexandria. After the initial discovery, the significance of the scrolls was explored by the Dominican Fathers of the famous French "Ecole Biblique," and now by biblical scholars the world over. Unlike the pattern of life prevailing in the Judaism of the Temple, this community observed poverty, chastity, and obedience as rigid disciplines and practiced a daily baptism. Admission to membership was highly selective. They flourished when the Christian movement was taking root and, while we still lack sufficient evidence, it is possible that the impact of this group and others like them was much stronger on Judaism (and thus on Christianity) than we had imagined before finding the scrolls.

THE FOUR GOSPELS

The main sources of information about Jesus of Nazareth are of course the four Gospels: Matthew, Mark, Luke, and John. Christians embrace both the Old and the New Testaments and find in the names and places of both Testaments the cherished points of their faith. Jesus is the center. The whole land has unique meaning through him. The great figures of the Old Testament lead up to him, and the apostles fan out from him. He is the promised Messiah, the Lord and Savior of all. The Holy Land is called holy because of him. Here he became incarnate; here he taught and healed; here he died and rose again for the salvation of the world. Little wonder that his followers, even 2000 years later, find this a land of enchantment and awe.

THE ANNOUNCEMENT TO ZECHARIAH

Where does the story of Jesus begin? With Bethlehem? With the announcement by the angel Gabriel to Mary? With the angel's appearance to Zechariah, telling him that he would yet father a son who "will go before the Lord in the spirit of Elijah?" Or does the story start far back in the dim beginnings when after the Fall into sin God told Satan that the seed of woman should bruise his head? The promise of a Messiah or Savior was repeated many times through the centuries, and the people of Israel lived in expectation of that fulfillment.

8

We might well begin with Zechariah as the immediate prelude to Christ's coming. For it was to this old priest that the angel promised a son, John the Baptist, who would prepare the way for the Messiah's coming.

THE ANNUNCIATION TO MARY

Soon after his appearance to Zechariah, the angel Gabriel appeared to a young girl, Mary, in the small town of Nazareth. The angel told Mary, "Behold, you will conceive in your womb and bear a son, and you shall call his name Jesus. He will be great, and will be called the Son of the Most High...and of his kingdom there will be no end."

Mary, greatly troubled, asked for an explanation. "The Holy Spirit will come upon you, and the power of the Most High will overshadow you; therefore the child to be born will be called holy, the Son of God."

Mary's response to the angel has echoed down the centuries as a fitting word for anyone called of God: "Behold, I am the handmaid of the Lord; let it be to me according to your word."

Beneath the magnificent Basilica of the Annunciation in Nazareth, which proudly proclaims the hidden mystery of the Incarnation, the visitor will see the humble grotto where it is believed Mary received the angel.

MARY VISITS ELIZABETH

Before leaving her, the angel informed Mary that her cousin, Elizabeth, the wife of Zechariah, was to have a child. "Mary went with

haste to a city of Judea and entered the house of Elizabeth." To go in haste from Nazareth to Judea in those days was a long and tedious, even perilous, journey. Mary probably avoided two of the three possible routes, since one was used by Roman soldiers and the other was a long detour through the Jordan valley. She probably went through Samaria, even though "the Jews had no dealings with the Samaritans." In any event, when she arrived she greeted Elizabeth with the news of the angelic visit in the beautiful words of the Magnificat, a hymn of praise so rhapsodic that it is still widely used in the prayers or liturgies of the church: "My soul magnifies the Lord, and my spirit rejoices in God my Savior."

When three months later Mary returned to Nazareth, Elizabeth gave birth to John. Of him his father Zechariah, filled with the Holy Spirit, said, "And you, child, will be called the prophet of the Most High; for you will go before the Lord to prepare his ways."

THE BIRTH OF JESUS

Perhaps no words in all Christendom have inspired such tenderness and even awe as this simple account by Luke: "In those days a decree went out from Caesar Augustus that all the world should be enrolled. This was the first enrollment when Quirinius was governor of Syria. And all went to be enrolled, each to his own city. And Joseph also went up from Galilee, from the city of Nazareth, to Judea, to the city of David, which is called Bethlehem, because he was of the house and lineage of David, to be enrolled with Mary, his betrothed, who was with child. And while they were there, the time came for her to be delivered. And she gave birth to her firstborn son and wrapped him in swaddling cloths, and laid him in a manger, because there was no place for them in the inn." The birth of this peasant child has given to the world its finest music and its most sublime art, and has released into the lives of people an unparalleled surge of joy and hope and love. Heaven came to earth, and the earth has never since been the same.

We who have sung Phillips Brooks' hymn, "O little town of Bethlehem, how still we see thee lie," may find it difficult to substitute a stable and a manger for the Church of the Nativity, built by Helena, the mother of Emperor Constantine and dedicated in A.D. 327, and in the 6th century enclosed by the larger structure under Justinian. But the Judean hills are the same and the stars shine at night. With a little imagination the enchanting story of the birth, angels, shepherds, the star, and the wise men can be reclaimed. Despite the jostling stream of pilgrim-visitors and the highly ornate interior of the basilica, to stand at the bare, stone entrance to the grotto is to journey back to the quiet night that changed the world.

THE PRESENTATION AT THE TEMPLE

The significance of the birth went unnoticed by most of the throng that came to Bethlehem for the census, but Joseph and Mary must have been overcome by the strange things that happened. They followed to the letter the customs of Judaism and had Jesus circumcised on the eighth day, and 33 days later presented him in the Temple. There a just and devout man named Simeon, seeing the baby, took him in his arms and broke out into these words of prophecy and prayer:

Lord, now lettest thou thy servant depart in peace,
according to thy word;
for mine eyes have seen thy salvation
which thou hast prepared in the presence of all peoples,
a light for revelation to the Gentiles,
and for glory to thy people Israel.

THE WISE MEN

Persuaded by strange signs that a great king was to be born, and led by a star, wise men or magi from the East came to adore and to bring gifts. Unfamiliar with the prophecies of Israel, they stopped in Jerusalem to ask King Herod about the newborn king. Herod's scribes, going back to the prophecies of Micah, directed them to Bethlehem, and the star led them to the stable. Warned in a dream not to let Herod know about the child, whom he intended to kill as a possible rival to his throne, the wise men returned to the East by a different route.

THE FLIGHT INTO EGYPT

Also in a dream, Joseph and Mary were instructed to flee with the child to Egypt and to remain there until Herod's death. Herod, meanwhile thwarted in his scheme, ordered the death of all boy babies in Bethlehem under two years of age. Upon the death of Herod, the holy family returned and lived in Nazareth.

JESUS' YOUTH

Only one incident is recorded in the childhood and youth of Jesus. No doubt he grew up as any other boy in Nazareth. At the age of 12 he went with his parents on the traditional pilgrimage to Jerusalem. On their return journey, Joseph and Mary discovered that Jesus was missing. Going back to the city, they found him in the Temple astonishing the doctors of the Law with his understanding.

While none of the Gospels dwell on Jesus' life in Nazareth, the village is rich with symbols. Here is the magnificent Basilica of the Annunciation built above the grotto where Mary is thought to have received the angel's message. Around the original grotto one can also see remains of an early Judeo-Christian place of worship, of a Byzantine church and a church built by the Crusaders in the 12th century. Nearby there is St. Joseph's church and in its crypt the probable site of the carpenter shop.

JESUS BEGINS HIS MINISTRY IN GALILEE

The public ministry of Jesus began with his baptism by John in the river Jordan (near Bethabara), when John pointed to him as "the lamb of God who takes away the sin of the world," and when a voice from heaven said, "This is my beloved Son in whom I am well pleased." Now about 30 years old, Jesus left Nazareth to wander as a teacher and healer for three years, and to be caught in the maelstrom of events that led to the cross. Once, upon his return to Nazareth, his people became enraged when he indicated that he was the Messiah. He narrowly escaped with his life.

12

The hub of his activity in Galilee was Capernaum, sometimes called "his own city," a town where Romans and Jews lived peacefully together. It had a harbor on the shores of the Sea of Galilee, and it lay on the famous "via Maris," the main artery linking Asia to Africa and Europe, close to the border of Roman Palestine. Only the ruins of this city survive, but we find the remains of two high walls of the ancient synagogue, beautifully carved stones, remnants of an octagonal Byzantine chapel with a mosaic floor representing fish scales, and a Judeo-Christian house of worship with pious symbols and inscriptions. Still lower there is the foundation of a first-century house with several rooms where two fish hooks were found, probably the home of Simon Peter's mother-in-law.

No city in the north could have been a more auspicious place for his teaching ministry, for here people of many nations were streaming through. Here he healed the centurion's servant, the man sick of the palsy, the man with the withered hand, Peter's mother-in-law, and many others.

Most of the "signs" and miracles occurred in the villages of Galilee. After calling his first disciples, he wandered with them from place to place, teaching and healing. His first "sign" was at a marriage feast in the town of Cana, where for the first time he "revealed his glory" by changing water into wine. The traditional site of this event is still to be seen below the church of the little village, near the road from Nazareth to Tiberias.

In the village of Nain he raised from the dead the only son of a widow as she was following his body to the grave. On the plains of Gennesaret he healed many sick who were brought to him. In a border town between Galilee and Samaria he healed 10 lepers, only one of whom came back to thank him, "and he was a Samaritan."

SEA OF GALILEE

Whatever else may have changed in 2000 years, this beautiful lake remains the same "Jewel of Galilee." Its waters flow in from northern
13 Lebanon and Mt. Hermon, and out into the river Jordan to the Dead

Sea. Here the first disciples plied their trade as fishermen; here the Lord stilled the storm; here he walked on the water; here sitting in a boat he spoke to the multitudes. Not far from its northern shore, near Bethsaida, he fed 5000 men "not counting the women and children" with five loaves and two fishes.

On one of the hills overlooking the lake he must have spoken the "Sermon on the Mount," a treasure house of superlative spiritual insights. The view stretches from the dainty chapel of the Beatitudes, from Golan to Galilee and down the Jordan Valley. To sit on the hillside and listen to the reading of these lines from Matthew 5 is an experience most pilgrims covet.

Blessed are the poor in spirit, for theirs is the kingdom of heaven.
Blessed are those who mourn, for they shall be comforted.
Blessed are the meek, for they shall inherit the earth.
Blessed are those who hunger and thirst for righteousness, for they shall be satisfied.

Blessed are the merciful, for they shall obtain mercy.
Blessed are the pure in heart, for they shall see God.
Blessed are the peacemakers, for they shall be called sons of God.
Blessed are those who are persecuted for righteousness' sake, for theirs
is the kingdom of heaven.
Blessed are you when men revile you and persecute you and utter all
kinds of evil against you falsely on my account. Rejoice and be glad,
for your reward is great in heaven, for so men persecuted the prophets
who were before you.

THE TRANSFIGURATION ON MT. TABOR

Most visitors to the north country will want to visit Mt. Tabor, thought
to be the high mountain where, in the presence of Peter, James, and
John, Jesus was "transfigured, and his face shone like the sun, and his
garments became white as light. And behold, there appeared to them
Moses and Elijah talking with him." The disciples were overcome with
wonder and proposed building three shrines. Suddenly a bright cloud
overshadowed them, and they heard a voice, "This is my beloved son,"
as at Jesus' baptism. When the cloud was gone, "They saw no one but
Jesus only."

Mt. Tabor is a dome-like mountain, ranging high over the valley of
Jezreel or Esdraelon. We reach the summit by a winding road, and at
the entrance to the plateau we face an ancient Crusaders' gate. We
walk through a lane of cypress trees to the basilica of native stone,
which was built between the two world wars of this century. The
basilica is divided into three naves, one for Moses, one for Elijah, and
one for Jesus. A beautiful mosaic above the central nave portrays the
scene of the Transfiguration. In the lateral chapels are frescoes of
Moses at Mt. Sinai and Elijah before Mt. Carmel.

This impressive mountain inspired the psalmist: "Tabor and Hermon
joyously praise thy name." And it was here that the prophetess
Deborah gathered 10,000 warriors from the tribes of Naphtali and
15 Zebulun and sent them into victorious battle.

MOUNT HERMON

It was in Caesarea Philippi at the foot of Mt. Hermon that Jesus addressed the question to his disciples, "Who do you say that I am?" and Peter answered, "You are the Christ, the Son of the living God." This dialogue is thought to have occurred at Banias (a pagan sanctuary to the idol Pan), one of the three sources of the river Jordan. Looking up at the high rocks, we see small niches from this heathen place of worship, associated with mythical water nymphs. This is one of the most beautiful places in the north.

Not far distant in Phoenicia, in the district of Tyre and Sidon, today's Lebanon, Jesus heard the persistent pleas of the Canaanite woman for her daughter and said, "O woman, great is your faith! Be it done for you as you desire." Her daughter was healed instantly.

JACOB'S WELL AT SICHEM

It was on one of his several pilgrimages to Jerusalem that Jesus stopped at Jacob's well in Samaria. A woman was drawing water and Jesus asked her for a drink. Surprised that a Jew would demean himself to ask a favor from a Samaritan, she entered into conversation with him, the outcome of which is one of the most moving episodes of the New Testament. Jesus uncovers her unsavory life; he reveals himself as "the water of life"; he tells her that God is not necessarily worshiped in one place, neither on the mountain in Samaria nor in Jerusalem, but that "true worshipers will worship the Father in spirit and in truth." Overwhelmed by Jesus, she hurried into the city and summoned people, "Come, see a man who told me all that I ever did. Can this be the Christ?"

The ancient well pointed out today as Jacob's well in Nablus (from *Nea-polis*, the new city, capital of Samaria) is most probably the one where Jesus and the woman met. In the Greek Orthodox crypt, below an uncompleted church (construction stopped in August 1914) one can still draw fresh water with rope and bucket.

16

Jesus most likely stopped more than once in the verdant, oasis-like city of Jericho. "As he drew near to Jericho, a blind man was sitting by the roadside begging; and hearing a multitude going by, he inquired what this meant. They told him, 'Jesus of Nazareth is passing by.' And he cried, 'Jesus, son of David, have mercy on me!' And Jesus said to him: 'Receive your sight; your faith has made you well.'"

Also at Jericho a rich tax collector, being short of stature, climbed into a sycamore tree to catch sight of Jesus. Seeing him, Jesus stopped and said, "Zacchaeus, make haste and come down, for I must stay at your house today." The people, who held tax collectors in contempt, thought it wrong for Jesus to single out this man. Zacchaeus, on the other hand, was honored, received him in his home with joy, and determined to change his manner of life. He told Jesus, "Behold, the half of my goods I give to the poor; and if I have defrauded anyone of anything, I restore it fourfold." And Jesus announced, "Today salvation has come to this house, since he is also a son of Abraham. For the Son of man came to seek and to save the lost."

Every Christian is familiar with Jesus' story told to a lawyer who asked, "And who is my neighbor?" "A man was going down from Jerusalem to Jericho, and he fell among robbers who stripped him and beat him, and departed, leaving him half dead. A Samaritan came to where he was...bound up his wounds...brought him to an inn, and took care of him." Having finished the story, Jesus turned to the lawyer and asked, "Which of these three, [two others had passed by] do you think, proved neighbor to the man?"

TEACHER-HEALER

Near the northern wall of Jerusalem is the pool of Bethesda, believed to have healing powers, especially when "an angel of the Lord went down and troubled the waters." In its five porticoes "lay a multitude of invalids, blind, lame, paralyzed. One man was there who had been ill for 38 years." Knowing that he had been there a long time, Jesus said to him, "Rise, take up your pallet, and walk." At once the man was healed.

On the opposite side of Jerusalem, on the southern slope of David's city, the Ophel, is the pool of Siloam, which is the outlet of Ezechias' tunnel. Here Jesus healed a man blind from his birth by anointing his eyes with a poultice of clay and spittle and telling him to wash in the pool. Receiving his sight, he fell down at Jesus' feet saying, "Lord, I believe."

One day in the Temple court Jesus came upon a mass of people about to stone a woman taken in adultery. They turned to Jesus, perhaps for his approval. Silently Jesus bent down and wrote with his finger on the ground. Then he said, "Let him who is without sin among you be the first to throw a stone at her." One by one the sullen crowd left and Jesus turned to the woman, "Woman, where are they? Has no one condemned you?...Neither do I condemn you; go, and do not sin again."

THE LAST JOURNEY

"And taking the twelve, he said to them, 'Behold, we are going up to Jerusalem, and everything that is written of the Son of Man by the prophets will be accomplished." The disciples, knowing the enemies that awaited him in the capital city, protested vigorously against his taking such a risk. But the die was cast. Isaiah had prophesied, "By his stripes we are healed," and now Jesus' hour had come. He was on his way to the cross.

Behind him were the more happy days in Galilee, where people adored him and followed him. In Jerusalem were people who feared him as an insurrectionist and who were plotting his death. Even the countryside provided contrast. From the lush Galilean land of fruit and water he now entered the harsh, barren hills of Judea.

Bethany is a village on the eastern slope of the Mount of Olives. Here, in the home of Mary and Martha, and Lazarus (whom he had raised from the dead), Jesus stayed at the opening of the Passover week. Today in Bethany one may see the ruins of a large Byzantine monastery, and an olive press, next to a modern church built later on this site.

On Sunday, the first day of the week which was to become the most important week in the history of the world, he sent two of his disciples on an errand. "Go into the village and you will find an ass tied, and a colt with her; untie them and bring them to me." Now he was ready for his triumphal Palm Sunday entrance into Jerusalem. Astride the donkey, he rode down from the Mount of Olives through the Kidron valley to the Temple area. During the Passover season Jerusalem thronged with devout pilgrims from many lands. In a burst of enthusiasm for someone rumored to be a king and a deliverer, people swarmed along his path, throwing their garments in the way, waving palm and olive branches, and cheering, "Hosanna to the Son of David! Blessed is he who comes in the name of the Lord."

THE MOUNT OF OLIVES

For the traveler who wants a panoramic view of Jerusalem, both the old and the new, there is no vantage point to compare with the Mount of Olives. This is a long ridge to the east of the city, separated from the city by the Kidron valley. Standing at the crest, we can survey the long history of the city. We identify the Ophel city of the Jebusites which was conquered by David from the Canaanite tribe seven years after he became king. We see Mt. Moriah, where Solomon built the house of the Lord. Also one can distinguish the city boundaries under the Herods, and later under the Crusaders. The massive walls were built by Suleiman the Magnificent in the 16th century. And surrounding the old city are the sprawling and soaring industrial and apartment complexes of modern Israel.

Below is the Kidron valley and the Garden of Gethsemane, and on the far side, Golgotha. Before going into the city, a person can well stand a long while on the Mount to meditate on the tragic and glorious events that will be recalled as he winds his way from one memorable site to another in the ancient walled city, scarcely more than 320 acres in area.

THE MONEY CHANGERS

Spurning the danger that faced him, Jesus was seen daily in the Temple, teaching and speaking in parables. In the outer court were "money changers," selling oxen, sheep, and pigeons to the pilgrims to be used for sacrifice. In a burst of indignation, he drove them out, overturning their tables, and said, "It is written, 'My house shall be a house of prayer' but you make it a den of robbers." His enemies were always hovering about, trying to find evidence to charge him with betrayal of either Roman or Jewish law. Showing him a coin, they asked, "Is it lawful to give tribute to Caesar, or not?" Avoiding the trap, he replied, "Render therefore to Caesar the things that are Caesar's, and to God the things that are God's."

MOUNT ZION

On Thursday of Holy Week, the eve of the Jewish Passover feast, Jesus gathered his disciples together for a final meal. They met in an upper room of a house on Mount Zion. As each disciple arrived, Jesus assumed the role of a household servant and washed his dusty feet, saying, "If I then, your Lord and Teacher, have washed your feet, you also ought to wash one another's feet. For I have given you an example, that you also should do as I have done to you." Later Paul was to write to the congregation in Philippi, "Have this mind among yourselves, which you have in Christ Jesus, who, though he was in the form of God,...emptied himself, taking the form of a servant." A ceremony of washing is still in the Maundy Thursday liturgies of some

Christian churches, where the highest dignitary of the church—in Jerusalem, the Patriarch—washes the feet of 12 persons.

During the meal "Jesus took bread, and blessed, and broke it, and gave it to the disciples and said, 'Take, eat; this is my body.' And he took a cup, and when he had given thanks he gave it to them, saying, 'Drink of it, all of you; for this is my blood of the covenant, which is poured out for many for the forgiveness of sins.'" Having instituted his "memorial," the sacrament of Holy Communion, he prayed, "Father, may they all be one even as we are one, I in them and thou in me, that they may become perfectly one."

The original upper room, called the *Cenacle*, was incorporated in the great Basilica built in the 4th century A.D. by Helena, and destroyed by the Persians in the early 7th century. The house was reconstructed in the Middle Ages (a Crusader's coat of arms is still to be seen on one of its walls) and was turned into a mosque in the 16th century by the Moslems. On its ground floor is the traditional tomb of David, considered by Islam as one of their great prophets. Only since 1948 have Christians had free access to this place.

GARDEN OF GETHSEMANE

After the supper, events rushed on to the grim climax. Judas, the betrayer, had slipped out to join the conspirators. The other disciples joined Jesus as he went down the eastern slope of Mt. Zion, through the Kidron valley, to a garden called Gethsemane. There he withdrew from them to pray alone. He cried, "My Father, if it be possible, let this cup pass from me; nevertheless, not as I will, but as thou wilt." Returning to his disciples, he found them sleeping, and said, "Why do you sleep? Watch and pray that you may not enter into temptation."

In the Garden today we see eight gnarled olive trees which may have been there at the time of Jesus. The splendid "Basilica of the Agony" is there, constructed after World War I by the Italian architect Barluzzi on the ruins of a 4th century church built by Emperor Theodosius. Inside is the rock on which Jesus may have prayed and suffered.

21

THE CAPTURE

A motley group of armed people led by Judas swarmed into the darkened Garden. Judas betrayed his master with a kiss, and the soldiers took Jesus away. Peter, who had sworn never to abandon him, stole toward the courtyard of the High Priest. Charged by a maid as Jesus' follower, Peter denied it vehemently three times. Jesus had predicted, "Before the cock crows, you will deny me three times." Suddenly Peter heard the cock crow, and in shame went out and wept bitterly. Saint Peter-in-Gallicantu, (St. Peter-at-the-cock-crow) is the church which recalls the denial and repentance of this great leader of the early church. Nearby, on the eastern slope of Mt. Zion, are ancient ruins believed to be the remnants of the High Priest's palace, and right next to the ancient terraced street leading down to the valley is a cistern venerated by Christians as the prison where Jesus was kept during the night.

TOWER ANTONIA

Early next morning, Good Friday, Jesus was ushered before the Roman Governor to stand trial. There, where the mighty Tower Antonia, the Lithostrotos or Gabbata, now stands, he faced Pontius Pilate. Pilate asked him, "Are you a king?" Jesus replied, "My kingship is not of this world; if my kingship were of this world, my servants would fight and deliver me. But for this I was born and for this I have come into the world, to bear witness to the truth. Everyone who is of the truth hears my voice." Pilate brushed aside the matter with the cynical remark, "What is truth?" But Jesus' adversaries were not to be put off, so to appease them Pilate ordered him scourged. The soldiers, amused by this strange prisoner, stripped him, put a scarlet robe on him, a crown of thorns on his head, a reed in his hand, then knelt before him and mocked him, "Hail, king of the Jews," and spat on him and struck him on the head with the reed.

Pilate told the rabble, "Behold, I am bringing him out to you, that you may know that I find no crime in him." Jesus came out wearing the robe and the crown of thorns. Pilate said, "Here is the man." The chief priests and officers pressed Pilate further with cries, "Crucify him. If you release this man, you are not Caesar's friend." Fearing a riot, Pilate sat down on the judgment seat and handed Jesus over to be crucified.

The Antonia fortress was a vantage point from which the Roman governor could oversee the huge courtyard of the Jewish people. If trouble seemed to be brewing among the seething crowd, Pilate could easily send down his soldiers to reestablish order. The very stones on which the trial took place may be seen today in the enclosure below the convent and pilgrims' hospice of the Sisters of Zion, still called the convent of the Ecce Homo (Latin for "Behold the man"). Some of the stones are marked with strange drawings, possibly games the soldiers played during leisure time or perhaps clues to the tortures they used on prisoners.

VIA DOLOROSA—THE WAY OF SORROWS

They led him away to crucify him. On the route, known as "The Way of Sorrows," he was given a massive wooden cross to carry to the small hill called Golgotha (*Har Hagolgolet* in Hebrew, "mount of the skull") outside of the Ephraim Gate of the city, the Roman place of execution. When Jesus crumbled under the weight of the cross, the soldiers snatched a sturdy man from the crowd, Simon of Cyrene, to carry it for him. Today we follow his route through the alley-like streets, with markers to denote each of the "stations" which indicate aspects of his sufferings: the cruelty of the soldiers, the indifference of the mocking crowds, the despair of his followers, the weeping of pious women, his stumbling and falling under the weight of the cross.

There they crucified him, on Golgotha, flanked on either side by two criminals. The soldiers cast lots for his garments. From the cross Jesus prayed, "Father, forgive them; for they know not what they do." It was now the sixth hour (about noon) and there was darkness over the whole land until the ninth hour (about 3 p.m.). Then Jesus, crying with a loud voice said, "Father, into thy hands I commit my spirit," bowed his head and breathed his last.

In an empty tomb, never before used, Jesus was buried. Joseph of Arimathea, a member of the Council who voted against Jesus' death, obtained special permission from Pilate to remove his body from the cross before the most solemn Sabbath should begin (Friday sundown) and bury it in his nearby cave-like grave.

It was an empty tomb that the women found early Sunday morning when they came with spices and perfumes to anoint his body. On Friday everything had seemed over for his followers. All that was left was to give the body proper care before they would drift back to Galilee. But everything was not over! The huge stone blocking the entrance to the tomb had been rolled away and the tomb was empty. Entering the grave, the women faced an angel dressed in white who said, "Do not be afraid; for I know you seek Jesus. He is not here; for he has risen, as he foretold." All the prophecies of the Old Testament, the many enigmatic statements of Jesus, and their own longings and yearnings now flowed into one overpowering fact: the Messiah was here! The great event of the Christian faith, the resurrection, had occurred.

Jesus appeared a number of times to his followers during the 40 days after his resurrection. Then one day at the Mount of Olives, in the presence of his disciples, he ascended to heaven. A short time later as his followers were gathered in an upper room for prayer, the Holy Spirit came upon them in tongues of fire. Jesus had promised this: "But you shall receive power when the Holy Spirit has come upon you; and you shall be my witnesses in Jerusalem and in all Judea and Samaria and to the end of the earth." The church of Jesus Christ was launched. Within a century it had encircled the Mediterranean. It leaped national boundaries and oceans and is today the faith of hundreds of millions on all continents of the earth.

THE HOLY LAND

Why should a country 140 miles long and between 30 and 70 miles wide, no larger than the state of New Jersey, be so important in the history of the world? Not because of its archaeological treasures; Egypt perhaps has more. Not because of its legacy in art and philosophy; Greece has given us more. Not because of its ancient world power; it was always buffeted among the mighty.

It is the land of the Bible. And the Bible inspires and records the faith of innumerable millions, now and through the centuries.

For the Christian the events and places and people of this land contain the history of God as he has dealt, and still deals, with the people of the earth. The Christian finds almost everything in this land suffused with transcendent meanings. This is where his Lord walked, where he taught, where he healed, where he suffered and died and rose again.

The Grotto of the Annunciation in Nazareth, the Grotto in Bethlehem, the Church of St. Peter-in-Gallicantu and the Church of the Resurrection (the Church of the Holy Sepulcher) in Jerusalem, together with all the other sites in Galilee, Samaria, and Judea will be no more than incidental sights to the curiosity seeker. But to the Christian, the believer, they set memory, imagination, and faith soaring.

It is not surprising that from the first century on, through the ill-conceived Crusades, and especially in more recent decades, pilgrims have come from all parts of the world to see with their eyes the places that have become dear to their faith. Churches and shrines have been built and destroyed and built again. Today restoration of the "holy places" is being carried on by peaceful agreement among the several religious communities that cherish this country's history.

IN THE FOOTSTEPS OF THE MASTER

It is hoped that this book will serve many. For those who have not visited this land, or never will, it will provide in superb pictures a review of the Bible account. For those who have been there, it will be a cherished souvenir. For others who may make the pilgrimage, it will be a splendid guide.

25

If you are fortunate enough to visit the land, you will not easily forget the reading of the Lord's Prayer on the very spot where it was first taught on the Mount of Olives, or the reading of the Sermon on the Mount as you are seated on the hillside overlooking the Sea of Galilee, or indeed your walk on the cobbled path where Jesus carried the cross up to Golgotha.

The sequence of pictures has been inspired by the Lord's command that his followers witness in Jerusalem, in Judea, in Samaria, and to the end of the earth. A special effort has been made to connect the different sites, shrines, and views from both the Old and the New Testaments.

May each of you who has this book in your hands find it an inspiration for your daily life. May it awaken in you a love for this country. Most of all, may it deepen your love for him who walked along its paths.

ALVIN N. ROGNESS

THE ILLUSTRATIONS

Jacket. Mount of Beatitudes, site of Sermon on the Mount, overlooking the Sea of Galilee.

Back Cover. Christmas Bells in Bethlehem. Judean Hills in the background.

Endpaper. Mosaic map of Madeba. The oldest existing map of the Holy Land, dating from the 6th century A.D. Byzantine period. Discovered in 1897. Jerusalem lies in the center of the map. Apart from depicting topographical details, such as mountains, towns, rivers, animals and vegetation, it bears Biblical inscriptions and alludes to essential events in the history of the Holy Land. It has taken artists a whole year to construct this map of 2.5 million mosaic stones.

Title page. The Land of Jesus. This attractive painting which decorates the apse of the Church of the Monastery of the Cross in Jerusalem exemplifies the conception expressed by Pope Gregory the First (c.600) in his letter to Serenus, the Bishop of Marseilles; "Pictures are used in the church, in order that those who are ignorant of letters may by merely looking at the walls read there what they are unable to read in books."
In a realistic manner, inspired by the iconographic tradition of the free Orthodox church, the artist shows the mystery of Christ and the beginning of the church, as perpetuated by the religious buildings and the holy places throughout the Holy Land. In the center is depicted the Monastery of the Holy Cross, itself, over which looms the figure of the crucified Christ. All around are the scenes of the Annunciation, the Nativity, the Magi, the Baptism of Christ, the Transfiguration and the Ascension. The prophet Elijah appears against the background of the Mar Elias Monastery.Two famous legends are illustrated in the foreground: A cypress tree growing through the monastery's roof, and Adam's skull at the foot of the Calvary (Golgotha). Painted c. 1770.

The landscape is highly stylized, almost Baroque. Artist anonymous.

Basket of bread between two fish. Mosaic depicting the miracle of the loaves and the fishes. From the Church of the Multiplication at Tabgha. Fifth century A.D.

7. Sculpture shows Christ, risen from death, inviting apostle Thomas to behold the wounds of his Passion (John 20:27).
Capitals found in the excavations around the Church of Annunciation, Nazareth. Carved in a very fine grained chalk stone, this is one of the most outstanding achievements of craftsmanship during the Crusaders' period. The influence of the style of French Burgundy is evident.

Jar from Qumran caves in which the Scrolls were kept. Israel Museum, Jerusalem.

Part of script from Isaiah read by Jesus in Nazareth Synagogue, found in Qumran caves, 1947.

. Madonna and Child. Pottery figurine found at Beth Shean. Byzantine period. Sixth century A.D.

11. "This is the place of the happy days." Greek inscription in mosaic floor, found in remnants of a monastery near Haifa, Sixth century A.D.

12. Inside the Church of the Resurrection, Jerusalem. In the last centuries this church was repeatedly and sometimes seriously damaged by earthquakes and fire. Disagreement among the different Churches sharing the building (Greek-Orthodox, Latin, Armenian, Coptic, Ethiopian, Syrian) prevented restoration. Only in very recent years was an understanding reached and this cooperation has produced outstanding results, as shown in this picture: one of the domes built originally by the Crusaders.

13. The Wheel of Fortune. Part of mosaic floor in the main foyer of the monastery at Beth Shean, 567 A.D.

14. Remnants of Byzantine church. Part of mosaic floor, depicting various birds and vegetation. Tabgha (Seven Springs). Early fifth century A.D.

15. Stone with ex-voto crosses. Crusaders' period. Found in the excavations near the Russian Church on the Mount of Olives, Jerusalem.

16. Bronze coin issued by the procurator Pontius Pilate, 30 A.D.

17. Roman soldiers give Jesus a drink of vinegar before his crucifixion at Golgotha. Mural painting in the Greek Orthodox Chapel at Golgotha, Holy Sepulchre, Jerusalem.

18. Pottery Lamp. Herodian period. Temple Mount excavations, Jerusalem.

19. The Last Supper. Part of a sculptured frieze from the Holy Sepulchre, Crusaders' period, twelfth century A.D. Jerusalem. Israel Department of Antiquities.

20. Small sun-dial. Herodian period. Temple Mount excavations, Jerusalem.

20. Ornamental architectural fragments. Herodian period. Temple Mount excavations, Jerusalem.

21. Angels feeding Daniel in the Lions' den. Mural painting in the Monastery of the Holy Cross, Jerusalem.

22. Detail of one of the Crusaders' capitals in the Church of Annunciation. Nazareth. According to old legend St. Matthew healed the son of the Ethiopian King, whose head is shown here.

23. Part of mosaic floor depicting fruit, birds and animals mentioned in the Old and New Testaments, in the Russian Church of Mary Magdalene, Mount of Olives, Jerusalem. Armenian craftsmanship. Uncovered 1871. Size 3,20 x 3,50 m., Fifth-sixth century A.D.

24. Armenian mosaic in the Russian Church, Mount of Olives, Jerusalem.

25. THE LAND OF THE BIBLE IN ROMAN TIMES" woodcut, original size 10,3: 12,4 cm., engraving by Abraham Pinaeus (Pinet), Geneva, 1560. Source: The Bible and Holy Scriptures, the English translation of the Genevan version.

The wilderness of Judah, rising from the Jordan valley at Jericho towards Jerusalem and Bethlehem, is deeply furrowed with ravines, canyons, and gorges. Because the rain falls on the western slopes of the Judean mountains, the eastern slopes remain a wasteland. At various times the Wilderness of Judah has served as a refuge and hide-out for fugitives from the authorities, for recluses, and for monastic sects at odds with society. This barren region is rich in associations with the history of the Holy Land and with crucial events in the life of Jesus.

A voice cries:
"In the wilderness prepare the way of the Lord,
make straight in the desert a highway for our God.
Every valley shall be lifted up,
and every mountain and hill be made low...
And the glory of the Lord shall be revealed." Isaiah 40:3-5

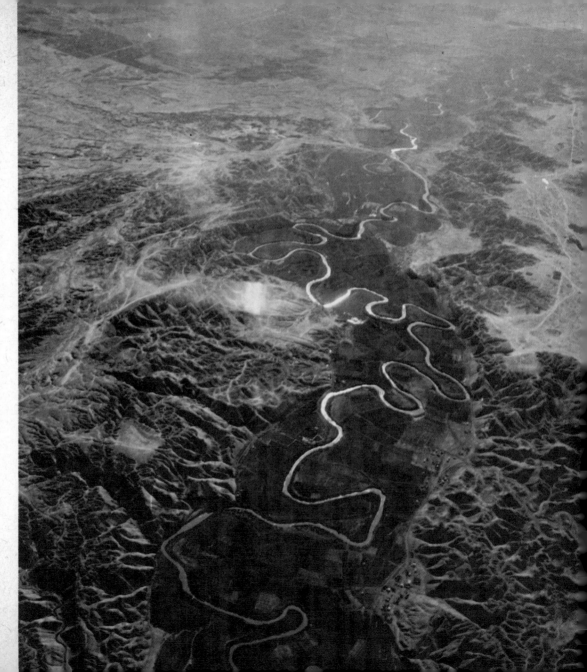

Bearing the memory of the Baptism, the river Jordan originates in the perpetual snows of Mt. Hermon, 9100 ft. above sea level, and winds along the valley bottom, ending at the Dead Sea, the lowest place in the world, 1300 ft. below sea level. The Jordan valley is the northern extremity of a great rift, running through the entire length of the Holy Land.

The Jordan's water reflects the subtle changes in the various landscapes scattered along its winding route. In the north it flows in clear fresh torrents through the fertile green valleys. It continues smoothly past the Wilderness of Judah and flows slowly through the salty, withered soil of the Dead Sea region.

It was here, at this bank of the Jordan, near Jericho, that the people of Israel crossed into the Promised Land after their 40 years in the desert (following page L.) and here too that John the Baptist baptized Jesus. From the 6th century A.D., a number of churches were built in the vicinity, dedicated to John the Baptist and the Baptism of Jesus. A traditional site of the Baptism is shown here.

In those days Jesus came from Nazareth of Galilee and was baptized by John in the Jordan.
Mark 1:9

2 | 3

Here in Qumran, a stone's throw from the Dead Sea, between 100 B.C. and about 60 A.D. lived a Jewish community identified by many with the Essenes. A sect that had completely withdrawn from the world in expectation of imminent salvation, the Qumranites saw themselves as the elect few who must live in penance and prayer. Their possible connection with John the Baptist and the early Christians has led to numerous and controversial speculations. Archaeological excavations at Qumran have discovered large numbers of cisterns, conduits from nearby springs, and baths, some of which seem to have been used for ritual immersion and sacramental purification. Two inkwells with dried ink in them indicate that the hall in which they were found was a *scriptorium*. In the Qumran caves the famous Dead Sea Scrolls were found, most of them in Cave No. 4 (preceding page R.).

The Dead Sea Scrolls of Qumran include fragments of almost all the books of the Old Testament and two well-preserved copies of the book of Isaiah, as well as other, previously unknown, texts, such as the "Manual of Discipline," which describes the regulation of the daily life of this first religious commune known to us, and the "Hodayot" Psalm (shown here). These scrolls are the oldest known biblical manuscripts. Jesus held a similar scroll in his hands when he read the passage of Isa. 61:1-2 in the synagogue of Nazareth and concluded: *Today this passage of the Scripture has been fulfilled in your hearing.* Luke 4:16-30

The scrolls were stored in jars carefully hidden in the caves, apparently with the intention of preserving them from the devastations of the 10th Roman Legion in 68 A.D. and recovering them later.

2000 years elapsed before a Bedouin shepherd sold to a cobbler in Bethlehem the "scraps of leather" he had found while tending his goats, which led the scholars to Qumran. Perhaps more scrolls will be discovered.

6 | 7

The lowest point on the face of the earth (1300 ft. below sea level) is called the Dead Sea because its mineral content is too high to support any living things.

Also called the Salt Sea and Lot's Sea (in Arabic, *Bakher Lot*), it is associated with the biblical stories of the destruction of Sodom and Gomorrah and with Lot's wife turning into a pillar of salt.

The Mountain of the Temptation in the Wilderness of Judah overlooks the green oasis of Jericho, which contains the 9000 year-old ruins of the oldest known city in the world. 1600 ft. above the Jordan Valley, this barren, steep mountain is thought to be the site of Jesus' 40 days of fasting. Here he faced the three temptations of Satan.

During the 300 years between the reign of Emperor Constantine and the Moslem invasion a large number of monasteries were built on the cliffs of this region. Today, there are still a few, such as St. Theodosius, St. Sabas and Quarantine, the Greek Orthodox monastery on the Mountain of the Temptation, whose communal refectories and strict disciplines are reminiscent of the way of life once conducted at Qumran. (R.).

Then Jesus was led up by the Spirit into the wilderness to be tempted by the devil. Matthew 4:1

10 | 11

The ruins of the Good Samaritan Inn, (preceding pages L. & R.) named after the Good Samaritan described in the New Testament, are located half-way between Jericho and Jerusalem. Now, as then, in the wilderness and on its periphery, the donkey and the camel are still commonly used for riding and as pack bearers.

> *A man was going down from Jerusalem to Jericho, and he fell among robbers, who stripped him and beat him, and departed, leaving him half dead...a Samaritan came, had compassion....* Luke 10:30–37

The picture opposite, with the church steeples on the Mount of Olives visible against the sky, may give some idea of what it must have felt like to come up out of the Wilderness and see signs of human habitation in the distance.

> *Behold, we are going up to Jerusalem.* Mark 10:33

Bethlehem, the birthplace of Jesus, lies on the edge of the wilderness (following pages L. & R.). Six miles south of Jerusalem on the road to Hebron, it reposes on a pair of peaks 2700 ft. above sea level. Its settlement dates back to antiquity. It is mentioned in the Egyptian Tel Amarna letters, as Beit Lahmu. In the Old Testament it is the small town in which King David was born. By the time of Herod's reign it had grown considerably. The city achieved world-wide fame as the site of the birth of Jesus. In 325 A.D. Queen Helena initiated the construction of the Church of the Nativity, which was completed by her son the Byzantine Emperor Constantine.

> *But you, O Bethlehem Ephrathah, who are little to be among the clans of Judah, from you shall come forth for me one who is to be ruler in Israel.* Micah 5:2; Matthew 2:6

Surrounded by vineyards, olive groves, pomegranate and fig orchards, the city of Bethlehem, with its white houses gleaming over the adjoining wilderness, is today as it has been for over a millenium, a focus of tourism and pilgrimage. The chiming of the famous Christmas Bells (L.) greets the thousands of pilgrims who come to Bethlehem every year to celebrate the birth of Jesus. Bethlehem is famous for its unique olivewood and mother-of-pearl crucifixes.

Bethlehem is familiar to members of all the monastic orders, like these Franciscan friars, meditating in a field near a local olive grove. Most of the churches in Bethlehem are dedicated to specific events related to Jesus' birth, like this Greek Chapel of the Shepherds' Field (R.). The traditional site of the angel's message to the shepherds heralding the birth of Jesus is located at Beth Sahour, a village where sheep still graze (following page L.).

...and there were in the same country shepherds abiding in the field, keeping watch over their flock by night.
Luke 2:8

17 | 18

On Christmas Day, the Latin Patriarch of Jerusalem and his entourage arrive in a solemn procession at the Basilica of the Nativity and Manger Square in Bethlehem, and are greeted by the local authorities and notables before entering the Basilica, seen here in the background (preceding page R.).

The fortress-like 4th century Basilica of the Nativity, the only Constantinian Basilica still existent in the Holy Land, (preceding page R.) stands just above the Grotto where Jesus was born. At the center of the Grotto itself stands the Altar of the Nativity, with the place of the Manger at its right (R.).

And this will be a sign for you: you will find a babe wrapped in swaddling cloths and lying in a manger.
Luke 2:12

21 | 22

Under the altar lies a star (L.), bearing the inscription *"Hic de Virgine Maria Jesus Christus natus"*: "Jesus Christ was born here of the Virgin Mary."

The star which they had seen in the East went before them, till it came to rest over the place where the child was. Matthew 2:9

The Midnight Mass, presided over by the Latin Patriarch of Jerusalem at the Church of the Nativity, is graced by the lighted text "Gloria in Excelsis Deo" and the traditional star.

For to us a child is born, to us a son is given: and the government will be upon his shoulder and his name will be called Wonderful Counselor, Mighty God, Everlasting Father, Prince of Peace. Isaiah 9:6

23 | 24

Bethany, the home of Lazarus, who was raised from the dead by Jesus, is 3 miles from Jerusalem on the easter
slopes of the Mount of Olives, at a place known today as el-Azariyeh. Remnants of three ancient churches, a
dedicated to Lazarus, are preserved side by side at the village's center. The grotto in the background, located next t
the white minaret, is believed to be the site of Lazarus' grave, giving its name to the Franciscan Church of Sai
Lazarus (in the foregroun

Six days before the Passover, Jesus came to Bethany, where Lazarus was, whom Jes
had raised from the dead. John 12

Bethphage is a small village on the Mount of Olives. The church in the foreground marks the starting point of the yearly Palm Sunday procession, recalling the triumphant entrance of Jesus to Jerusalem.

Hosanna to the Son of David! Blessed be he whom comes in the name of the Lord! Hosanna in the highest.
Matthew 21:9

25 | 26

The ancient soil still responds generously to those who till it. Workers in the hill countries of Judea, Galilee and Samaria, who still use the same age-old methods of their forefathers, are a living illustration of life in biblical times.

Varieties of fruit, vineyards, and orchards grow in abundance in Judea and Samaria. They are mentioned frequently in the Bible, especially in the Song of Solomon and in the Psalms. The grape, fig, pomegranate, olive, and date are mentioned in the parables of Jesus.

*I went down to the nut orchard, to
look at the blossoms of the valley, to
see whether the pomegranates were
in bloom.* Song of Solomon 6:11

I am like a green olive
tree in the house of God.
I trust in the steadfast
love of God for ever and
ever. Psalm 52:8

Throughout the centuries the same methods have been used for producing oil. This ancient olive press, which dates back to the Middle Ages, gives us a clear idea of these ancient techniques. It is to be seen in Bethany, in the Franciscan Convent near St. Lazarus Church.

Ein Kerem, "The Vineyard Spring," is the home of John the Baptist. Today it is a picturesque suburb about six miles from Jerusalem's center. Here John lived with his father Zechariah and his mother Elizabeth, Mary's cousin. At the center of the village stands the Church of John the Baptist (photo's center) marking the traditional Grotto, the site of the house of Zechariah, where John was born (following page R.).

In those days Mary arose and went with haste into the hill country, to a city of Judah, and she entered the house of Zechariah and greeted Elizabeth. Luke 1:39

Entrance gate to the
Church of the Visitation. A
beautiful mosaic at the
church's facade depicts
Mary's visitation.

*My soul magnifies
the Lord, and my
spirit rejoices in
God my Savior.*
Luke 1:46

The Grotto of John the Baptist's birth.

And all these things were talked about through all the hill country of Judea.
Luke 1:65

The inscription on the altar in this grotto of the Baptist's nativity:

Hic Praecursor Domini Natus Est: This is the birthplace of the forerunner of the Lord.

Jerusalem, the Eternal City cherished by three great religions, crowns the Judean hills 2500 ft. above sea level. It was the scene of some of the most significant events in the life of Jesus: The Last Supper, his agony in Gethsemane, his trial, his way to the cross, his crucifixion, resurrection, and ascension.

And I saw the holy city, new Jerusalem, coming down out of heaven from God...and I heard a great voice from the throne saying: Behold, the dwelling of God is with men. He will dwell with them, and they shall be his people. Revelation 21:2

Preceding page L.: The Temple area. The Old City is alternately surrounded by valleys, Kidron to the east and Hinnom to the west and south, and protected by hills, of which the highest is Mt. Scopus (2700 ft.) to the north and the Mount of Olives to the east (R.). To the south (corner R.) can be seen Mt. Ophel, which shelters the remnants of the Old City of David, dating back to the Israelite period.

The massive stone walls, adorned with seven gates, were built by the Ottoman ruler Suleiman the Great (1540), over the ruins of older walls. Enclosed are very narrow lanes leading through crowded bazaars and awe-inspiring shrines. In the foreground is the Damascus Gate; at center right background, the dome of the Church of the Holy Sepulcher. At center left background towers the steeple of the Lutheran Church of the Redeemer.

I was glad when they said to me, "Let us go to the house of the Lord!" Our feet have been standing within your gates, O Jerusalem! Psalm 122:1–2

| 41

The Citadel, David's Tower. Location of Herod's Palace. The city walls (L.).

Upon your walls, O Jerusalem, I have set watchmen; all the day and all the night they shall never be silent. You who put the Lord in remembrance, take no rest, and give him no rest until he establishes Jerusalem and makes it a praise in the earth. Isaiah 62:6

Tunnel leading from the Fountain of Gihon to the pool of Siloam, an outstanding achievement under the reign of King Hezekiah (8th century B.C.). This was the main water supply to the city. It is also associated with Christ's curing of the blind.

42 | 43

Esplanade of the Temple,
view from the Dome of the
Rock towards the Christ-
ian Quarter, showing the
tower of Redeemer Church
and the domes of the
Church of the Holy Sepul-
chre. (L.).

*And he was teaching
daily in the temple.*
Luke 19:47

Esplanade of the Temple,
the Arches of Judgment.
According to Moslem trad-
ition, here will hang the
scales weighing the good
and bad deeds of the faith-
ful. In the background the
Ecce Homo dome.

The narrow and crowded street of the Arab "Souk," the bazaar (L. & R.), within the walls of the Old City.

Miniature model of the Second Temple, built on the grounds of the Holyland Hotel, on the outskirts o
Jerusalem. All available scientific data have been used for this unique reconstruction, which gives the bes
idea of Jerusalem's Temple at the time of Jesus
Huge Herodian stone, part of the Western Wall, most venerated place of worship for the Jews. This wal
surrounds and sustains the artificial plateau, Herod's enlarging of the Temple Mount (R.

A view from the plaza of the Temple Mount, *Mount Moriah* towards the Mount of Olives. The *Dome of the Rock* (Mosque of Omar) built in the 7th century A.D. by Abd-el-Malik on the very site of the First and Second Temples, as a super-structure over the Holy Rock. In the background, the Mount of Olives with the Russian Chapel of St. Mary Magdalene, the Chapel "Dominus Flevit," the "Tower of the Ascension" and the Carmelite Convent "Our Father."

Archaeological excavations at the southern wall of the Temple Mount (R.).

Do not trust in these deceptive words: This is the temple of the Lord, the temple of the Lord, the temple of the Lord.
Jeremiah 7:4

50 | 51

Liturgy in St. James Armenian
Cathedral near Mt. Zion. This 12th
century church houses religious and
artistic treasures of the Armenian
people.

> *Oh send out thy light and thy*
> *truth; let them lead me, let*
> *them bring me to thy holy hill*
> *and to thy dwelling!*
> Psalm 43:3

The valley of Hinnom (Gehenna),
south of Mt. Zion, with the Greek
Orthodox monastery built on the
site of Hakeldama (the potter's field)
(L.).

> *They took counsel, and bought*
> *with them the potter's field, to*
> *bury strangers in. Therefore*
> *that field has been called the*
> *Field of Blood to this day.*
> Matthew 27:7

The tomb of Mary. An Armenian
monk descending the steps on the
slope of the Mount of Olives past
the beautiful icons on the way to the
tomb cut into the rock, where,
according to tradition, Mary was
buried by the Apostles.
(following page R.).

52 | 53

Greek Orthodox ceremony of the "washing of the feet," the Thursday before Easter. (Preceding page R.).

Then he poured water into a basin, and began to wash the disciples' feet, and to wipe them with the towel with which he was girded. John 13:5

Mount Zion with Dormition Abbey on its peak (L.). "In a large upper room" on this mount Jesus ate the Passover meal with his disciples. The Cenacle—the Last Supper Room—is to be found next to the Dormition Abbey. This mountain is believed by Jews and Moslems to be the burial place of King David.

The Room of the Last Supper, Mt. Zion (R.).

"...and tell the householder, 'The Teacher says to you, Where is the guest room, where I am to eat the Passover with my disciples?' And he will show you a large upper room furnished; there make ready." Luke 22:11-12

The ancient staircase leading from Mt. Zion to the Kidron Valley (L.), a portion of a Roman street which Jesus passed on his way from the Cenacle to Gethsemane, on the evening before his trial. In the background, the Assumptionist Church of St. Peter-in-Gallicantu, the traditional location of the palace of the high priest Caiaphas.

And he came out, and went, as was his custom, to the Mount of Olives; and the disciples followed him. Luke 22:39

St. Peter-in-Gallicantu, the so-called "Prison of Christ."

And Peter remembered the saying of Jesus, "Before the cock crows, you will deny me three times." And he went out and wept bitterly. Matthew 26:75

The Kidron Valley at the foot of the Mount of Olives: the Church of Gethsemane, or the Agony of the Lord, to the left, and Absalom's tomb to the right. Nearby are other ancient tombs, dating back to times when, according to tradition, the dead were buried outside the city's walls.

When he came to the place he said to them, "Pray that you may not enter into temptation."
And he withdrew from them about a stone's throw, and knelt down and prayed. Luke 22:39

The Church of Christ's Agony looking across the Garden of Gethsemane and the Kidron Valley towards the walls of the Temple Mount.

After the Last Supper, Jesus went forth with his disciples across the Kidron Valley, where there was a garden, which he and his disciples entered.
John 18:1

The Golden Gate. Outside this wall, a Moslem cemetery (R.).

Lift up your heads, O gates! and be lifted up, O ancient doors! that the King of glory may come in.
Psalm 24:7

In the Church of Geth-
semane. Above the altar, a
mosaic showing the Lord
praying; at the foot of the
altar, a part of the original
rock on which, according
to an old tradition,
he actually prayed.

*And being in an
agony he prayed more
earnestly; and his
sweat became like
great drops of blood
falling down upon the
ground.*
Luke 22:44

Centuries-old olive trees in the Garden of Gethsemane.

Then Jesus went with them to a place called Gethsemane, and he said to his disciples, "Sit here, while I go yonder and pray."
Matthew 26:36

Russian Church of St. Mary Magdalene on the slopes of the Mount of Olives, above the Garden of Gethsemane.

Mary Magdalene went and said to the disciples, "I have seen the Lord," and she told them that he had said these things to her.
John 20:18

View of the Old City through the window of the "Dominus Flevit" Chapel (R.).

And when he drew near and saw the city he wept over it.
Luke 19:41

66 | 67

Via Dolorosa, the Way of Sorrows, also called "The Way of the Cross"; street sign in Latin, Arabic, and Hebrew (L.).

Via Dolorosa, Greek-Orthodox "Way of the Cross" procession (R.).

Look and see if there is any sorrow like my sorrow which was brought upon me. Lamentations 1:12

The excavations at the Pool of Bethesda, near St. Anne's Crusader Church (L.).

Now there is in Jerusalem by the sheep gate a pool, in Hebrew called Bethesda, which has five porticoes. In these lay a multitude of invalids, blind, lame, and paralyzed.
John 5:2

Via Dolorosa. The "Ecce Homo" arch.

So Jesus came out, wearing the crown of thorns and the purple robe. Pilate said to them, "Here is the man!"
John 19:5

Palm Sunday procession, leading down the slopes of the Mount of Olives towards Gethsemane and the walls of the Old City (L. & R.).

They took branches of palm trees and went out to meet him, crying, "Hosanna! Blessed is he who comes in the name of the Lord...."
John 12:13

Via Dolorosa. Sisters coming to join the Roman Catholic "Way of the Cross" procession under the leadership of the Franciscan Fathers of the Custody of the Holy Land.

He who does not take his cross and follow me is not worthy of me.
Matthew 10:38

Starting point of the Way of the Cross in the yard of the Moslem el Omaria school, built on the site of the Roman fortress "Antonia," the residence of the Roman governor of Jerusalem, traditional place of Jesus' trial (R.).

And they bound him and led him away and delivered him to Pilate the governor.
Matthew 27:2

74 | 75

Convent of the Sisters of Sion (Church of the Ecce Homo): stones of the Roman courtyard, the Lithostrotos (L.).

> *They led Jesus from the house of Caiaphas to the praetorium. It was early. They themselves did not enter the praetorium.*
> John 18:28

Detail of an ancient stone of the courtyard (R.), showing the cruel "Game of the King," played by Roman soldiers. This may have some connection with the scourging and mockeries inflicted on Jesus.

4th Station of the Way of the Cross: Jesus encounters his mother.

Simeon said to Mary his mother, "Behold, this child is set for the fall and the rising of many in Israel, and for a sign that is spoken against (and a sword will pierce through your own soul also) that thoughts out of many hearts may be revealed. Luke 2:33–35

6th Station of the Way of the Cross, at the chapel of the Little Sisters of Jesus: Veronica wipes the blood-stained face of Jesus (R.).

He had no form or comeliness that we should look at him, and no beauty that we should desire him. He was despised and rejected by men; a man of sorrows, and acquainted with grief; as one from whom men hide their faces. Isaiah 53:2

Pilgrims carrying a
heavy wooden cross on
Good Friday along the
Way of Sorrows "Via
Dolorosa"
(preceeding page L.).

*Far be it from me to
glory except in the cross
of our Lord Jesus Christ,
by which the world has
been crucified to me, and
I to the world.*
Galatians 6:14

Mount Calvary,
Golgotha.
(Preceeding page R.).

*So they took Jesus, and
he went out, bearing his
own cross, to the place
called the place of a
skull, which is called in
Hebrew Golgotha.*
John 19:17

Greek Orthodox Patriarch of Jerusalem, Benediktos, at the Gate of the Church of the Resurrection, the Crusader Basilica of the Holy Sepulcher, is led by an impressive procession out of this church, in which both Mount Calvary and the tomb of Christ are remembered (L.).

The "Anastasis," place of Christ's tomb, in the Church of the Holy Sepulcher.

Interior of the tomb of Christ in the Church of the Resurrection (following page L.).

The Chapel of the Copts at the rear of the "Anastasis" (Overleaf R.).

> *And Joseph took the body, and wrapped it in a clean linen shroud, and laid it in his own new tomb which he had hewn in the rock; and he rolled a great stone to the door of the tomb.*
> Matthew 27:59

The Garden Tomb, also known as Gordon's Calvary.

> *Now in the place where he was crucified there was a garden, and in the garden a new tomb*
> *where no one had ever been laid. John 19:41*

The Greek Orthodox Monastery of the Holy Cross, built on the spot where, according to a pious tradition, the
tree grew, the wood of which was to be the Lord's cross (L.).

The location of Christ's Ascension to heaven in the foreground, and view of the Old City of Jerusalem from the top of the Mount of Olives.

As they were looking on, he was lifted up, and a cloud took him out of their sight. And while they were gazing into heaven as he went, behold, two men stood by them in white robes, and said, "Men of Galilee, why do you stand looking into heaven? This Jesus, who was taken up from you into heaven, will come in the same way as you saw him go into heaven." Acts 1:9–11

Qubeibeh, in the hills of Judah, one of the possible locations of the village Emmaus. Remnants of the ancient Roman highway (R.).

That very day two of them were going to a village named Emmaus, about seven miles from Jerusalem, and talking with each other about all these things that had happened. While they were talking and discussing together, Jesus drew near and went with them. Luke 2:13

View of the ruins of Caesaria Maritima, built by Herod the Great in honor of Caesar Augustus. Later one of the harbors used by the Crusaders (L.).

Caesarea was the residence of the Roman procurators. In 1961 this stone was excavated, bearing the inscription:...S TIBERIEUM ...(PON)TIUS PILATUS ...(PRAEFE)CTUS JUDA(E). (Building erected in honor of Emperor Tiberius by Pontius Pilate, Prefect of Judah).

They led him away and delivered him to Pilate the governor.
Matthew 27:2

The ancient town of Shechem is located about 6 miles northwest of present-day Nablus on the main route from Judea to Galilee. This route passes by Mounts Gerizim and Ebal, which rise above the Valley of Patriarchs, associated with God's promise to Abraham.

To your descendants I will give this land.
Genesis 12:7

In the unfinished Greek Orthodox church (L.) standing near the ruins of ancient Shechem, is the well (R.), where, according to tradition, Jesus spoke with the woman of Samaria.

Jesus said to her, "Every one who drinks of this water will thirst again, but whoever drinks of the water that I shall give him will never thirst; the water that I shall give him will become in him a spring of water welling up to eternal life."
John 4:13–14

The fertile land of Galilee, northern part of the Holy Land, is a patchwork of valleys and mountains, woods and open fields, torrents and rivers. Within it are important landmarks in the life of Jesus: Nazareth, place of the Annunciation; the shores of the Sea of Galilee, scene of his public life; and Mt. Tabor, the mountain of the Transfiguration. In Galilee Jesus performed his first miracles and began to preach. From the local villagers, he selected his disciples.

Cana in Galilee, associated with Jesus' miracle of the wine, is 5 miles east of Nazareth (R.). Several churches, all commemorating the first "sign," are located in the village alongside the remnants of some built in the 4th century. The Greek Orthodox church with its famous vineyard is one.

On the third day there was a marriage at Cana in Galilee, and the mother of Jesus was there; Jesus also was invited to the marriage, with his disciples. When the wine failed, the mother of Jesus said to him, "They have no wine."…. This, the first of his signs, Jesus did at Cana in Galilee, and manifested his glory; and his disciples believed in him. John 2:1,11

The Mountain of the Transfiguration, Mt. Tabor, which towers 2000 ft. above sea level, overlooking the plain of Jezreel, is located nine miles southwest of Nazareth. On a clear day, one can view the beautiful landscape from Mt. Hermon in the east to the sea in the west. (Also p.100).

Jesus took with him Peter and James and John his brother, and led them up a high mountain apart. Matthew 17:1

The Basilica of the
Transfiguration.
Remnants of
Crusaders'
monastery are
scattered nearby.

*Lo, a bright cloud
overshadowed
them, and a voice
from the cloud
said, "This is my
beloved Son, with
whom I am well
pleased, listen to
him."*
Matthew 17:5

Detail of the mosaic picture above the main altar (R.) in the Basilica of the Transfiguration, with its three naves (L.).

And he was transfigured before them, and his face shone like the sun, and his garments became white as light. And behold, there appeared to them Moses and Elijah, talking with him.
Matthew 17:2–3

ET TRANSFIGVRATVS EST ANTE EOS

Nazareth, located on a mountain above the Jezreel valley, where the Annunciation occurred and where Jesus spent his youth and early adulthood, attracts pilgrims from all over the world (preceding page R.). In those days the town was small and quite unknown. Today it ranks with Jerusalem and Bethlehem as an important place in Jesus' life.

The dome of the Church of the Annunciation towers high above the picturesque rooftops. It was rebuilt in 1966 on the ruins of the Byzantine Basilica, built by Constantine in 337, and the Crusader Church.

The angel Gabriel was sent from God to a city of Galilee named Nazareth, to a virgin betrothed to a man whose name was Joseph, of the house of David; and the virgin's name was Mary. And he came to her and said, "Hail, O favored one, the Lord is with you."
Luke 1:26–28

The site of the synagogue in which, according to tradition of the 6th century, Jesus prayed and proclaimed himself sent by God.

And he came to Nazareth, where he had been brought up; and he went to the synagogue, as his custom was, on the Sabbath day. Luke 4:16

Inside the Basilica of the Annunciation, the crypt facing the Grotto (L.). The inscription below the altar of the Grotto:

VERBUM CARO HIC FACTUM EST.
(Here the Word became flesh).

In the beginning was the Word,
and the Word was with God,
and the Word was God.

He was in the beginning with God;
all things were made through him,
and without him was not anything made that was made.
In him was life, and the life was the light of men.
John 1:1–4

Ancient Jewish tomb below the school of the Sisters of Nazareth (L.).

Who will roll away the stone for us from the door of the tomb? Mark 16:3

Mary's Well in the Greek Orthodox Church of St. Gabriel.

Behold, you will conceive in your womb and bear a son, and you shall call his name Jesus. Luke 1:31

Nazareth, the "Souk" (market) (following pages R. & L.). Street leading to the Greek Catholic Church (in the background).

And he went and dwelt in a city called Nazareth, that what was spoken by the prophets might be fulfilled, "He shall be called a Nazarene." Matthew 2:23

The smooth surface of the sea of Galilee reflects the surrounding mountains. In the days of Jesus it was named the Sea of Gennesaret. In the villages along its shores Jesus performed many miracles.

More densely populated in those days, it was a center for shipping, fishing, trade, and craftsmanship.

Tiberias (L.), built by Herod Antipas in honor of Emperor Tiberius. In the foreground is the tomb of Rabbi Meir-Baal-Haness, just above the famous Tiberias hot springs.

After this Jesus went to the other side of the Sea of Galilee, which is the Sea of Tiberias.
John 6:1

Sea of Galilee, pilgrims listening to the word of God.

In those days, when again a great crowd had gathered, and they had nothing to eat, he called his disciples to him, and said to then, "I have compassion on the crowd, because they have been with me now three days."
Mark 8:1–2

Ruins of the ancient synagogue, built of basalt stone, at Chorazin, north of Capernaum, on the shores of the Lake of Galilee (L.). Jesus had rebuked the people of Chorazin who had rejected him.

Woe to you, Chorazin! Woe to you, Bethsaida! for if the mighty works done in you had been done in Tyre and Sidon, they would have repented long ago in sackcloth and ashes.
Matthew 11:21

The "Seven Springs" Chapel at Tabgha on the shores of the Sea of Galilee.

112 | 113

Capernaum, the ruins of the ancient synagogue, with details of crowns, eagles, David's hexagram, menorah, and a palm branch, etched in stone relief. During the life of Jesus it was called "his own city," the place he chose as his headquarters for preaching and teaching. Here he performed many of his miracles.

And they went into Capernaum; and immediately on the Sabbath day he entered the synagogue and taught. And they were astonished at his teaching, for he taught them as one who had authority. Mark 1:21-22

Fishermen hauling in their catch, the famous St. Peter's fish, (preceding page R. & L.).

"Master, we toiled all night and took nothing! But at your word I will let down the nets." And when they had done this, they enclosed a great shoal of fish; and as their nets were breaking, they beckoned to their partners in the other boat to come and help them. Luke 5:5–7

The Mount of the Beatitudes (overleaf L.), the site of the "Sermon on the Mount," overlooking the Sea of Galilee.

Seeing the crowds, he went up on the mountain...And he opened his mouth and taught them. Matthew 5:1–2

Overleaf R.: Local villagers watching the fishing boats.

And passing along by the Sea of Galilee, he saw Simon and Andrew the brother of Simon casting a net in the sea...And Jesus said to them, "Follow me." Mark 1:16–17

The river Jordan, flowing down from Mount Hermon towards the Sea of Galilee (Overleaf last page).

ΑΙΝѠΝΕΝΘΑ
ΝΥΝΟCΑΠCΑ
ΦΑC
ΒΕΘΑΒΑΡΑ
ΓΑΛΓΑΛΑ ΤΟ ΚΑΙ
ΔѠΔΕΚΑΛΙΘΟΝ
ΙΕΡΙΧѠ
ΓΟΦΝΑ
ΚΛΗΡ
ΒΕΝΙΑΜΙΝ
ΒΕΘѠΡѠΝ
ΟΙ ΜΑΚΚΑΒΑΙΟΙ